Italian

Introduction

Food and culture are essential and a way of life in Italy and is the heart of the family and what brings families together is eating good food with quality ingredients.

Even a simple dish with only a few good quality ingredients can be one of the best and memorable dishes you have ever eaten and is simple to make.

Included in this book are the best basic recipes that Italians love to cook and eat with their families.

From pasta to chicken, meat, or fish are the usual choices, along with Lasagna, which we all eat today with great pleasure, is among the oldest Italian dishes.

BENVENUTO IN ITALIA

BUON APPETITO

Cooking Pasta

To cook pasta, bring 3.5 L (7 ½ pints) salted water to a brisk boil.

Add a small amount of pasta at a time. If you are cooking spaghetti, hold it near the end and gently lower the other end into the boiling water; it gradually softens and curves around the pan as it enters the water.

Boil pasta briskly, uncovered, stirring occasionally until just tender.

The Italians call it 'al dente' – the pasta should be firm when bitten between the teeth. Do not overcook.

Drain in a colander, rinse with hot water and stir through a dash of olive oil and salt (optional).

Tips

- When cooked, immediately drain the pasta.

- Don't rinse it, unless the directions specifically say so, as washing reduces the nutrients in the meal.

- Always sauce the pasta at once to keep it from sticking, tossing well to distribute the sauce evenly.

- Pasta that is to be sauced and baked should be undercooked slightly, otherwise it will be too soft after baking.

- With spaghetti, apply a light sauce to a fine stick, such as angel-hair, and a more robust sauce to a thicker strand.

- A rule of thumb is to ensure the sauce grades increase with the thickness of the spaghetti, linguine or fettuccine used.

- When using tubular pasta, try a clinging sauce that will stick both inside and out.

- Shell-shaped pasta is just right for holding puddles of sauce and pieces of meat, fish or poultry.

- Twists are more versatile as they allow a robust sauce to wrap around them for a full–taste dish, and can accept a light vinaigrette when served in a cold salad.

- Sauce ingredients are only limited by your imagination and desire to experiment.

Tomato Toasts with Fresh Basil

Serves 4

4 tablespoons olive oil
1 teaspoon mixed dried herbs
freshly ground black pepper
1 baguette, cut into 12 slices
8 Roma or plum tomatoes
1 clove garlic, crushed
25g (¾ oz) sun-dried tomatoes in oil, drained and finely chopped
1 teaspoon vinegar
1 teaspoon sugar
2 tablespoons fresh basil, chopped

🫒 Preheat the oven to 220°C (430°F).

🫒 Combine 3 tablespoons of the oil with the dried herbs and pepper and season well.

- Brush both sides of each bread slice with the flavoured oil. Cook for 8 minutes or until lightly golden and crisp.

- Meanwhile, put the tomatoes in a bowl, cover with boiling water and leave for 30 seconds.

- Peel and deseed, then roughly chop the flesh.

- Heat the remaining olive oil in a frying pan and add the garlic, chopped tomatoes, sun-dried tomatoes, vinegar, sugar and basil.

- Cook, stirring occasionally, for 5 minutes or until heated through.

- Remove from the heat. Pile the tomato mixture on top of the toasts, season and serve.

Garlic Bread

Serves 4

1 French bread
2 cloves garlic, peeled and crushed
250 g (8 oz) butter

Preheat oven to 220°C (430°F).

With a sharp knife, cut bread into slices almost to the bottom, being careful not to sever the slices.

In a small bowl, mash garlic thoroughly into butter. Spread garlic butter generously on both sides of bread slices. Wrap bread loosely in aluminium foil, place in the oven for 10–15 minutes, and bake until bread is crisp and golden.

Serve hot.

Insalata Caprese

Serves 2-4

400 g (14 oz) Roma tomatoes, thickly sliced
250 g (8.8 oz) bocconcini/fresh mozzarella, sliced
½ cup fresh basil leaves, shredded
¼ cup extra-virgin olive oil
2 tablespoons balsamic vinegar
sea salt and freshly ground black pepper

 Arrange tomatoes, bocconcini, and basil leaves on individual plates.

 Drizzle with olive oil and balsamic vinegar, and sprinkle with sea salt and freshly ground black pepper.

 Serve with crusty bread.

Baby Octopus Salad

Serves 4

12 baby octopuses
2 teaspoons coriander seeds, toasted
2 cloves garlic, finely minced, plus 12 cloves, sliced
2 tablespoons lemon juice
¼ cup sweet chilli sauce
2 cucumbers, peeled
1 large red capsicum (bell pepper)
1 bunch watercress
1 cup pickled ginger
1 tablespoon black sesame seeds
1 cup coriander (cilantro) leaves
1 cup bean sprouts
250 ml (8 fl oz) canola oil
pinch of sea salt

- Clean octopuses by peeling off skin and removing heads.

- Grind toasted coriander seeds in a mortar and pestle.

- Combine coriander, minced garlic, lemon juice, and sweet chilli sauce in bowl. Add octopus and marinate in refrigerator for 2 hours.

- Using a vegetable peeler, peel thin strips of cucumber. Thinly slice bell pepper lengthwise. Combine watercress, cucumber, bell pepper, pickled ginger, sesame seeds, cilantro leaves and bean sprouts in a large bowl. Set aside.

- Heat oil in a heavy-based skillet and fry sliced garlic until golden brown and crispy. Remove and drain on a paper towel.

- Strain marinade from the octopus into a small saucepan and bring to simmer. Set aside to cool and use as dressing later.

- Heat a wok and stir-fry octopus until cooked, approximately 3–4 minutes. Combine prepared salad with octopus and toss with dressing. Season to taste.

Minestrone

Serves 6

4¼ cups chicken stock
440g (15oz) canned peeled tomatoes, chopped
2 cups dry white wine
2 onions, diced
3 carrots, diced
1 turnip, diced
2 sticks celery, sliced
2 red bell peppers (capsicums), diced
1 large courgette (zucchini), sliced
440g (15oz) canned red kidney beans, drained
¾ cup penne
½ teaspoon ground turmeric
salt and freshly ground black pepper

Pesto

1 bunch fresh basil, handful of leaves kept aside to garnish
3 cloves garlic, crushed
60g (2oz) Parmesan cheese, finely grated
½ cup olive oil
salt and freshly ground black pepper

- Place the stock, tomatoes, wine, onions, carrots, turnip, celery and bell peppers in a large saucepan. Bring to the boil, reduce the heat and simmer for 20 minutes.

- Add the courgette, kidney beans, penne and turmeric. Simmer for a further 40 minutes, stirring regularly, until the vegetables are tender. Season with salt and pepper.

- To make the pesto place the basil, garlic and Parmesan in a food processor or blender.

- Blend until finely chopped.

- While the motor is running, gradually add the olive oil through the feed tube until a paste is formed. Season with salt and pepper.

- Serve the soup in large soup bowls, topped with 1 tablespoon of pesto and basil leaves.

Beef Carpaccio

Serves 4

500 g (1 lb) beef fillet
3 tablespoons extra-virgin olive oil
salt and freshly ground black pepper
125 g (4 oz) rocket (arugula)
1 tablespoon balsamic vinegar
pecorino cheese shavings

- Use a sharp knife, slice the beef into 5 mm (0.2 in)-thick slices. Lightly oil a sheet of baking paper & season it lightly with salt & freshly ground pepper.

- Place 4 slices of beef on this, approximately 5 cm (2 in) apart. Place another oiled piece of baking paper on top, & gently pound the meat until it has spread out to at least twice its former size. Repeat with remaining meat slices. Refrigerate until needed.

- Arrange the beef slices around the rocket. Drizzle with balsamic vinegar and remaining olive oil.

- Serve, topped with shavings of cheese & more black pepper.

Lasagne

Serves 6

24 sheets instant lasagne*
60g (2oz) mozzarella cheese, grated

Cheese sauce

75g (2½oz) butter
⅓ cup all-purpose (plain) flour
2 cups milk
90g (3oz) tasty cheese (aged Cheddar), grated freshly
ground black pepper

Meat sauce

2 teaspoons vegetable oil
2 onions, chopped
2 cloves garlic, crushed
1.25kg (2lb 12oz) ground beef
2 x 440g (15oz) canned diced tomatoes
¾ cup red wine
2 tablespoons chopped mixed herbs
freshly ground black pepper

*No pre-cooking required

To make cheese sauce, melt butter in a saucepan over a medium heat. Stir in flour and cook, stirring, for 1 minute.

Remove pan from heat and whisk in milk. Return pan to heat and cook, stirring, for 4–5 minutes or until sauce boils and thickens. Stir in cheese and black pepper to taste and set aside.

Preheat the oven to 180°C (350°F).

To make meat sauce, heat oil in a skillet over a medium heat. Add onions and garlic and cook, stirring, for 3 minutes or until onions are soft.

Add beef and cook, stirring, for 5 minutes or until beef is brown.

Stir in tomatoes, wine and herbs, bring to simmering point and simmer, stirring occasionally, for 15 minutes or until sauce in reduced and thickened.

Season to taste with black pepper.

Line the base of a large greased baking dish with 6 lasagne sheets.

- Top with one quarter of the meat sauce and one-quarter of the cheese sauce. Repeat layers to use all ingredients, ending with a layer of cheese sauce.

- Sprinkle top of lasagne with mozzarella cheese and bake for 30-40 minutes or until it is hot and bubbling and the top is golden.

Tuna Lasagne

Serves 4

15g (½ oz) butter
2 sticks celery, finely chopped
1 onion, chopped
9 sheets instant lasagne*
400g (14oz) canned tuna, drained and flaked
2 tablespoons grated tasty cheese (aged Cheddar)
1 teaspoon curry powder
½ teaspoon ground sweet paprika

Curry Sauce

2 cups milk
1 cup water
30g (1oz) butter
⅓ cup all-purpose (plain) flour
2 teaspoons curry powder
2 eggs, beaten
2 tablespoons grated tasty cheese (aged Cheddar)
freshly ground black pepper
Sliced tomato for topping

*No pre-cooking required

🍒 To make the sauce, combine the milk and water and set aside.

🍒 Melt the butter in a saucepan, stir in the flour and curry powder and cook for 2–3 minutes.

🍒 Remove the pan from the heat and whisk in the milk mixture.

🍒 Return the sauce to the heat and cook, stirring constantly, for 4–5 minutes or until the sauce boils and thickens.

🍒 Remove the pan from the heat and whisk in the eggs and cheese. Season to taste with black pepper.

🍒 Set aside.

🍒 Preheat the oven to 180°C (350°F).

🍒 Melt the butter in a skillet and cook the celery and onion for 4–5 minutes or until onion is soft.

- Spoon a little sauce over the base of a lightly greased, shallow, ovenproof dish.

- Top with 3 lasagne sheets and spread over half the tuna and half the celery mixture, then a layer of sauce. Repeat layers, finishing with a layer of lasagne, then sauce.

- Combine the cheese, curry powder and paprika, and sprinkle over the lasagne.

- Slice tomato slices and lay on top.

- Bake for 30–35 minutes or until the noodles are tender and the top is golden.

Penne with Tomato Sauce

Serves 4

1 tablespoon extra virgin olive oil
1 red onion, finely chopped
2 sticks celery, finely chopped
2 cups canned chopped tomatoes
1 tablespoon tomato paste
1½ cups vegetable bouillon
1 cup cherry tomatoes, halved
1 teaspoon golden sugar
sea salt and freshly ground black pepper
1½ cups penne
4 tablespoons crème fraîche (optional)

- Heat the oil in a large, heavy-based saucepan.

- Add the red onion and celery and cook, uncovered, for 5 minutes over a medium heat until the vegetables are tender.

- Add the chopped tomatoes, tomato paste and bouillon and bring to the boil.

- Simmer, uncovered, for 15 minutes, stirring occasionally, until reduced and thickened.

- Add the cherry tomatoes, and sugar and season generously, then stir gently for about 3 minutes until heated through.

- Meanwhile, cook the pasta in plenty of boiling salted water until tender but still firm to the bite, then drain.

- Pour the sauce over the pasta, toss gently to avoid breaking the cherry tomatoes and serve with a dollop of crème fraîche (if using).

Spaghetti Carbonara

Serves 4

250–375 g (8–12 oz) spaghetti
2 tablespoons olive oil
3 slices bacon, finely diced
2 eggs
45 g (1½ oz) Parmesan cheese, grated
250 ml (8 fl oz) fresh cream
freshly ground black pepper, to taste

- Add spaghetti into boiling, salted water and cook for 8 minutes or until al dente.

- Just before spaghetti is ready, heat oil and fry bacon. In a bowl, beat in eggs and add cheese.

- Drain pasta and return to the hot saucepan. Add cheese mixture, cream, plenty of black pepper and crisp bacon. Mix well. Place the saucepan over a low heat for a minute or so, stirring constantly.

- Place in a hot dish and serve immediately.

Penne with Pancetta & Tomatoes

Serves 4

4 tablespoons extra virgin olive oil
200g (7oz) unsmoked pancetta or rindless lean bacon, roughly chopped
1 teaspoon crushed dried chillies
100ml (3½fl oz) dry white wine
1 sweet or mild onion, very finely chopped
salt
400g (14oz) canned chopped tomatoes
400g (14oz) penne
90g (3oz) Parmesan cheese, freshly grated

- Heat 2 tablespoons of the oil in a large, heavy-based skillet, then fry the pancetta or bacon and chillies for 2–3 minutes until the fat starts to run out.

- Add the wine and boil for 2–3 minutes or until reduced by half.

- Lower the heat, add the onion and ½ teaspoon of salt to the pancetta and cook, covered, for 8 minutes, stirring occasionally, until the onion has softened.

- Stir in the tomatoes and cook, covered, for 20–25 minutes or until thickened. If the mixture is a little dry, add 2 tablespoons of hot water.

- Season if necessary.

- Meanwhile, cook the pasta in plenty of boiling salted water until tender but still firm to the bite. Drain, then transfer to a warmed serving bowl.

- Stir in the remaining oil and half the sauce. Mix, then add 4 tablespoons of Parmesan.

- Toss, then spoon over the rest of the sauce and serve with the remaining Parmesan.

Spaghetti with Mussels

Serves 4

2kg (4lb 6oz) mussels
½ cup extra virgin olive oil
340g (12oz) spaghetti
100ml (3½fl oz) dry white wine
60g (2oz) chopped fresh parsley
2 cloves garlic, chopped
1 teaspoon crushed dried chillies

- Scrub the mussels under cold running water, pull away any beards and discard any mussels that are open or damaged.

- Place 2 tablespoons of the oil in a large, heavy-based skillet, then add the mussels. Cook, covered, shaking the skillet frequently for 2–4 minutes or until the mussels open. Discard any mussels that do not open.

- Reserve 12 mussels in their shells for garnishing.

Italian pasta

- Detach the remaining mussels from their shells and set aside. Discard the shells.

- Cook the pasta in plenty of boiling salted water until tender but still firm to the bite, then drain. Meanwhile, place the remaining oil, the wine, parsley, garlic and chilli in a large, heavy-based skillet and bring to the boil.

- Cook for 2 minutes to boil off the alcohol.

- Stir the mussels and pasta into the oil and chilli mixture and toss for 30 seconds to heat through.

- Serve garnished with the reserved mussels.

Spaghetti Bolognese

Serves 4

1 tablespoon olive oil
250 g (½ lb) minced beef
1 clove garlic, crushed
1 large onion (or 2 small onions), finely grated
500 g (1 lb) peeled tomatoes, chopped
1 teaspoon oregano or basil
1 teaspoon salt
freshly ground black pepper, to taste
1 teaspoon sugar
3 tablespoons tomato paste
250 ml (8 fl oz) beef stock
250 g (½ lb) spaghetti
Parmesan cheese, to garnish

Heat oil in frying pan, add meat, garlic and onion
and brown lightly.

- Add tomatoes, oregano, salt, pepper and sugar. In a small bowl, blend tomato paste with stock. Add this to mixture in frying pan.

- Simmer for 30 minutes, uncovered, so that sauce thickens slightly.

- When sauce is almost ready, cook spaghetti in boiling salted water until tender. Drain spaghetti, and place on a hot serving dish or plate.

- Pour hot sauce over spaghetti and sprinkle with Parmesan cheese. Serve additional cheese in a small bowl.

Spaghetti with Meatballs

Serves 4

Meatballs

4 slices white bread
500 g (1 lb) minced chuck or round steak
1 tablespoon Parmesan cheese, grated
1 tablespoon parsley, chopped
1 tablespoon onion, grated
2 teaspoons salt
¼ teaspoon black pepper
¼ teaspoon oregano
1 egg
3 tablespoons olive oil
250 g (8 oz) spaghetti or thin spaghetti
Parmesan cheese

Tomato Sauce

1 x 500 g (1 lb) can whole tomatoes
250 ml (8 fl oz) Italian tomato sauce
125 g (4 oz) tomato paste
60 ml (2 fl oz) water
60 ml (2 fl oz) red
wine (or water)
2 bay leaves, crushed
2 tablespoons parsley, chopped
1 clove garlic, crushed

- To make tomato sauce, combine all ingredients in a large saucepan. Simmer until thick, stirring occasionally for about 10 minutes.

- To make meatballs, place bread in a small bowl, add enough water to cover, and let stand for 2 minutes. Remove bread and squeeze out excess water.

- In a larger bowl, combine bread with minced steak, Parmesan cheese, parsley, onion, salt, pepper, oregano and egg.

- Mix lightly until thoroughly combined. Shape into small balls. Heat oil in a frying pan and brown meatballs on all sides.

- Add meatballs to sauce and simmer for 15–20 minutes.

- Meanwhile, cook spaghetti in salted, boiling water (about 20 minutes). Drain spaghetti and place on a hot serving dish or plate.

- Top with meatballs and sauce and sprinkle with Parmesan cheese.

Mussels with Garlic

Serves 6

72 mussels in their shells, washed
1 L (2 pints) water
250 g (8 oz) butter
salt and freshly ground black pepper, to taste
2 cloves garlic, finely chopped
2 tablespoons parsley, chopped
fine dry breadcrumbs

- Place mussels and water in a steamer and steam mussels open by shaking them over a high flame. Keep mussels in half shell and arrange on a platter.

- In a saucepan, melt butter, then add salt and pepper, garlic and parsley. Drizzle butter over mussels. Sprinkle with breadcrumbs and place under a preheated hot grill until brown. Serve at once.

Whitebait

Serves 4

sunflower or peanut oil for deepfrying
5 tablespoons all-purpose (plain) flour
salt and freshly ground black pepper
½ teaspoon cayenne pepper
1 teaspoon ground coriander
400g (14oz) frozen whitebait, defrosted, rinsed and
dried
½ cup flat-leaf parsley & lemon wedges

- Heat the oil in a deep saucepan, to check that the
  oil is hot enough for frying, drop in a cube of bread.
  Meanwhile, place the flour in a large plastic bag
  & add ½ teaspoon of salt, black pepper, cayenne
  pepper and coriander.

- Shake to mix, then add the whitebait to the bag a few
  at a time and shake gently to coat. Fry the whitebait in
  batches for 4–5 minutes, until crisp and golden.

- Sprinkle the whitebait with salt and serve with the
  deep-fried parsley and lemon wedges.

Veal Saltimbocca

Serves 4

4 veal escalopes, about 125g (4.4oz) each
2–3 tablespoons butter
250g (8.8oz) mozzarella cheese, sliced into 8 rounds
8 slices prosciutto
bunch sage, 2 teaspoons of it roughly chopped
½ cup dry white wine
¼ cup chicken stock

- Using a meat mallet, pound the veal until thin.

- Heat the butter in a pan, add the veal, and brown quickly, on both sides. Remove from pan, top each with 2 slices mozzarella, 2 slices prosciutto and 2–3 sage leaves. Secure together with toothpicks. Under a hot grill, grill veal for approximately 2 minutes, until cheese has just started to melt. Set aside.

- Reheat butter, add the chopped sage and cook for 1 minute. Add the wine and stock & reduce the sauce slightly. Pour the sauce over the veal, and serve immediately. Garnish with sage leaves.

Cannelloni Stuffed With Ricotta In Tomato Sauce

Serves 4-6

12 cannelloni tubes
3 cups ricotta cheese
2 eggs
4 shallots (scallions), finely sliced
60 g (2 oz) Parmesan cheese
salt and freshly ground black pepper, to taste
pinch of ground nutmeg
4–6 large ripe tomatoes, skinned and chopped
3 tablespoons olive oil
60 g (2 oz) butter

- Preheat oven to 180°C (350°F). Cook cannelloni according to packet instructions. Set aside until ready to fill.

- In a bowl, mix ricotta cheese, eggs, spring onions and ¼ cup Parmesan cheese thoroughly. Season with salt, pepper and nutmeg.

- Place tomatoes in a saucepan and cook, uncovered, until they are a thick pulp, stirring occasionally. Remove from heat and stir in oil gradually.

- Drain cannelloni and fill with ricotta cheese mixture. Place filled cannelloni side by side in a single layer in a buttered shallow baking dish.

- Pour tomato sauce around and over the cannelloni, sprinkle with remaining Parmesan cheese and dot with butter.

- Bake in the oven until bubbling, about 20 minutes. Serve at once.

Fettuccine Alfredo

Serves 6

250 g (8 oz) fettuccine
125 g (4 oz) butter
125 g (4 oz) Parmesan cheese, grated
¼ teaspoon salt
freshly ground black pepper, to taste
250 ml (8 fl oz) fresh cream
parsley, finely chopped and extra Parmesan cheese, to garnish

- Cook fettuccine for 15 minutes, or until al dente, in a large saucepan of rapidly boiling, salted water.

- Meanwhile, melt butter in a large saucepan, then add Parmesan cheese, salt, pepper and cream. Cook over a low heat, stirring constantly, until blended.

- Drain fettuccine. Immediately add to cheese mixture and toss until pasta is well coated. Place in a heated serving dish, sprinkle with parsley and Parmesan cheese and serve at once.

Gnocchi

Serves 4

3 medium-sized potatoes, washed
125 g (4 oz) plain (all-purpose) flour, sifted
1 egg
1½ teaspoons salt
extra flour
Italian Tomato Sauce or Bolognese Sauce
Parmesan cheese, grated, to garnish

- Boil unpeeled potatoes until tender. Peel while hot and place in a mixing bowl.

- Mash potatoes straight away, adding sifted flour, a little at a time, while potatoes are still hot. Add egg and salt and beat until smooth.

- Turn onto a well-floured board. Knead, working in enough flour to form a smooth, soft, non-sticky dough.

- Divide dough into several parts.

- Roll each to pencil thickness. Cut into 2 cm (¾ in) pieces. With the tines of a floured fork, press each piece so that it curls. Place on waxed paper.

- Sprinkle lightly with flour. Cook immediately, or within 2 hours.

- Add gnocchi a little at a time to a large pan of rapidly boiling salted water with a little oil added. Cook for about 5 minutes, or until gnocchi comes to the surface.

- Drain and keep warm in a heated bowl until all gnocchi is cooked.

- Serve in Tomato Sauce or Bolognese Sauce, sprinkled with Parmesan cheese.

Gnocchi

In the Italian tradition gnocchi are always meant to be dumplings.

They are generally made from a potato base with the addition of flour.

The proportions of potatoes and flour may vary from one region to another.

Clam Chowder

Serves 6-8

255g (9oz) butter
6 rashes of bacon, finely chopped
3 onions, finely chopped
1½ cups finely chopped celery
1 cup plain flour
4 cups milk
3 cups fish stock
500g (1lb) potatoes, finely diced
1kg (2lb) clam meat
salt and pepper
cream (optional), to serve

- Heat the butter in a saucepan and cook the bacon, onion and celery until tender.

- Add the flour and cook for 2 minutes.

- Add milk, fish stock and potatoes, cover and simmer for 10 minutes.

- Add the clam meat and cook again for 10 minutes. Season to taste.

- Serve in a deep plate with cream and parsley.

Tuna and Rice Bake

Serves 4

750 ml (1½ pints) water
1¼ cups uncooked brown rice, well washed and drained
⅓ cup shallots (scallions), chopped
1 egg, lightly beaten
1 teaspoon curry powder
1½ tablespoons butter, melted

Filling

1 x 425 g (13½ oz) can tuna in brine, drained
(reserve liquid)
1 carrot, grated
1 zucchini (courgette), grated
60 g (2 oz) butter
30 g (1 oz) cup flour
1 teaspoon mustard powder
1 teaspoon paprika, plus extra to garnish
½ teaspoon freshly ground black pepper
375 ml (12½ fl oz) milk
2 tablespoons parsley, chopped
2 teaspoons lemon juice
60 g (2 oz) tasty cheese, grated
thin lemon slices & chopped parsley, to garnish

- In a large saucepan, bring water to the boil. Slowly add rice. Stir once with a fork, then cover tightly with a lid. Simmer gently until all liquid is absorbed (45–50 minutes).

- Preheat oven to 200°C (375°F). In a bowl, combine cooked rice with shallots, egg, curry powder and butter. Press onto base and sides of a 23 cm (9 in) square ovenproof dish.

- Spread tuna evenly over rice base. Top with carrot and zucchini and set aside.

- Melt butter in a saucepan, then add flour, mustard, paprika and pepper and cook for 1 minute, mixing well.

- Gradually blend in milk and reserved tuna liquid, and bring mixture to the boil. Then add parsley and lemon juice, and stir until smooth.

- Pour sauce over vegetables, and sprinkle over cheese and paprika. Bake in the oven for 30 minutes until heated through.

- Serve garnished with lemon slices and chopped parsley.

Shrimp Risotto

Serves 4

500 g (1 lb) shrimp
4 tablespoons olive oil
2 small onions, finely chopped
1 tablespoon green peppercorns
250 g (½ lb) arborio rice
180 ml (6 fl oz) dry white wine
1 medium size onion, grated
squeeze lemon juice
chopped parsley & zest of 1 lemon, to garnish

🫒 Shell shrimp and make fish stock by boiling shells in about 970 ml (2 pints) water to which a pinch of salt has been added.

🫒 Strain and reserve liquid.

🫒 Chop shrimp and set aside.

- Place 2 tablespoons oil in a frying pan and lightly brown onions.

- Add green peppercorns and rice and cook, stirring constantly, until rice is lightly browned.

- Add wine.

- When wine has evaporated, add stock, gradually. Stir very lightly and simmer gently, uncovered, until rice is cooked. Add a little hot water or more wine if rice gets too dry.

- Meanwhile, heat remaining oil in a saucepan and add grated onion, lemon juice and chopped shrimp.

- Fry lightly until onion is translucent and shrimp are cooked – approximately 3 minutes.

- Stir through rice and serve sprinkled with parsley and lemon zest.

Roasted Pumpkin Risotto

Serves 4

500g (17½oz) butternut pumpkin, peeled and cut into
2cm (0.8in) pieces
2 tablespoons olive oil
2 teaspoons balsamic vinegar
salt and freshly ground black pepper
5 cups vegetable stock
1 onion, finely chopped
3 cloves garlic, crushed
2 cups arborio rice
1 teaspoon dried rosemary leaves
125g (4oz) goat's cheese, crumbled
150g (5oz) baby spinach leaves, washed and trimmed
¼ cup fresh parsley, chopped

 Preheat the oven to 220°C (430°F).

- Combine the pumpkin, 1 tablespoon olive oil, balsamic vinegar, salt and pepper in a non-stick baking tray.

- Bake in the oven for 20–25 minutes or until the pumpkin is golden.

- Meanwhile, place the vegetable stock in a saucepan. Bring to a boil and simmer gently.

- Heat the remaining oil in a large saucepan over medium heat. Cook the onion and garlic for 2–3 minutes or until soft. Add the rice and stir until combined.

- Add 1 cup of the stock and the rosemary leaves. Cook, stirring from time to time, until all the liquid is absorbed. Repeat this until all the stock is used and the rice is tender.

- Stir in the pumpkin, goat's cheese, baby spinach and parsley and season to taste. Cook until heated through and the spinach has wilted. Serve immediately with crusty bread.

Risotto with Spinach & Gorgonzola

Serves 6

4 cups vegetable stock
2 tablespoons olive oil
2 cloves garlic, crushed
1 onion, finely chopped
2 cups Arborio rice
½ cup white wine
150g (5oz) baby spinach
220g (8oz) Gorgonzola cheese, in small pieces
salt and freshly ground black pepper

- Place stock in a saucepan and bring to the boil. Leave simmering.

- Heat oil in a large saucepan, add garlic and onion, and cook for 5 minutes, or until soft.

- Add rice, and stir, until well coated.

- Pour in wine, and cook, until the liquid has been absorbed.

- Add a ladle of the stock, stir continuously, until the liquid has been absorbed, then add the next ladle of stock.

- Keep adding stock this way, and stirring, until all the stock is used, and until the rice is cooked, but still a little firm to bite.

- Add the spinach, cheese and seasonings. Stir and cook until spinach is just wilted and cheese has melted.

- Serve immediately.

Mushroom Risotto

Serves 4

90g (3oz) butter
1 onion, finely chopped
1 clove garlic, crushed
250g (9oz) mushrooms, sliced
2 cups Arborio rice
½ cup dry white wine
1 tablespoon tomato paste
1¼ cup vegetable stock, heated
Parmesan cheese

- Place butter in frying pan, add onion & garlic & cook until onion is golden.

- Add mushrooms & cook over low heat for 2 mins. Add rice to the saucepan & cook over a medium heat, stirring constantly, for 3 minutes or until rice becomes translucent. Add wine & tomato paste, stirring until absorbed. Pour half a cup of hot stock into rice mixture and cook, stirring constantly, until liquid is absorbed.

- Continue cooking in this way until all the stock is used.

- Remove from heat, add Parmesan and toss with fork to blend.

Seafood Risotto

Serves 6

125 ml (4 fl oz) olive oil
2 cloves garlic, chopped
1 medium onion, chopped
660 g (1½ lbs) arborio rice
1 bunch shallots (scallions), chopped
1 bunch fresh coriander (cilantro), chopped
4 pieces butternut pumpkin, cooked
1 L (2 pints) fish stock
250 ml (8 fl oz) white wine
1 kg (2 lb) marinara mix
¾ cup Parmesan cheese, grated
salt and freshly ground black pepper, to taste
3 tablespoons sour cream

- Heat oil in a large saucepan and gently fry onion and garlic.

- When onion is translucent, add rice. Stir well, until rice is coated with oil. Add shallots and coriander and cook for a few minutes, then add pumpkin.

- Add 250 ml (1 cup) stock, stirring constantly until it is absorbed.

- Add 250 ml (1 cup) wine and continue to stir.

- Continue to add stock by the cup (and stir regularly), until all stock is absorbed. It will take about 30 minutes to get the rice to an almost cooked stage.

- When rice is almost cooked, fold in the marinara mix and cook for a further 5 minutes.

- Add Parmesan. Season with salt and pepper. Cook for another few minutes, until seafood is done, then stir in sour cream.

- Serve in bowls, and sprinkle the last of the Parmesan on top.

Mussel Risotto

Serves 4

2 tablespoons olive oil
1 onion, finely chopped
2 cloves garlic, finely chopped
1 red bell pepper (capsicum), diced
1½ cups Arborio rice
2½ cups dry white wine
1kg (2lb 4oz) mussels, cleaned
1 sprig rosemary, leaves removed and chopped
2 sprigs thyme, leaves removed and stalks discarded
45g (1½oz) Parmesan cheese, grated

Place oil in a saucepan over medium heat. Add onion, garlic and bell pepper and cook for 2 minutes. Add rice and half the wine, stirring constantly until liquid is absorbed. Add mussels and the other half of the wine.

Add herbs, cover and cook until rice and mussels are cooked, stirring frequently. Discard any mussels that do not open.

Serve sprinkled with grated Parmesan.

Ravioli

Serves 6

Filling

2 tablespoons olive oil
375 g (12 ½ oz) minced beef or shredded chicken
250 g (8 oz) cooked spinach or frozen spinach, thawed
2 eggs, beaten
1 tablespoon Parmesan cheese
¾ teaspoon salt
¼ teaspoon freshly ground black pepper
500 g (1 lb) basic pasta dough
Italian tomato sauce
grated Parmesan or Romano cheese, to garnish

- To make filling, heat oil in a frying pan. Add meat and cook until browned, then place meat in a bowl.

- Prepare and cook spinach, draining it well.

- Finely chop spinach and mix with meat. Add eggs, Parmesan cheese, salt and pepper. Mix well. Set aside until ready to use.

- Divide pasta dough into quarters.

❧ Roll each quarter until it is 3 mm (⅛ in) thick, and a rectangular shape. Cut dough lengthways (using a pastry cutter, if you have one) into strips 12 cm (5 in) wide.

❧ Place 2 teaspoons of filling in the centre of one half of the pastry every 8.5 cm (3½ in), then fold over the other half covering the filling. Seal the whole strip by pressing the long edges together with the tines of a fork. Press the two layers of pastry together between the mounds of filling and cut in the middle between mounds with the pastry cutter, again sealing the cut edges with the tines of a fork.

❧ Add ravioli gradually, about a third at a time, to a large saucepan of rapidly boiling, salted water.

❧ Cook for 20 minutes or until tender.

❧ Remove with a slotted spoon. Drain well.

❧ Serve topped with heated tomato sauce and sprinkled with Parmesan cheese.

Veal with Mozzarella

Serves 4

750 g (1½ lb) veal steak, thinly sliced
seasoned flour
1 egg, beaten with 60 ml (2 fl oz) water
90 g (3 oz) fine breadcrumbs mixed with 30 g (1 oz)
Parmesan cheese, grated
olive oil, for frying
2 tablespoons extra olive oil
2 cloves garlic, crushed
1 onion, finely chopped
1 x 470 g (15 oz) can tomatoes, peeled
3 tablespoons tomato paste
¼ teaspoon dried thyme
½ teaspoon caster (superfine) sugar
salt and freshly ground black pepper, to taste
250 g (8 oz) mozzarella cheese, thinly sliced

- Preheat oven to 180°C (350°F). Flatten veal slices lightly, using the side of a meat mallet.

- Dip in seasoned flour, then in combined egg and water, and then coat with combined breadcrumbs and Parmesan cheese. Press crumbs on firmly.

- Heat oil in a frying pan and fry veal until golden brown on both sides. Drain on absorbent paper.

- Heat extra oil in a saucepan, then add garlic and onion and sauté for 5 minutes. Add tomatoes, tomato paste, thyme, sugar and salt and pepper. Cover, and simmer for 10 minutes.

- Pour one-third of tomato mixture into an ovenproof casserole dish. Arrange veal on top, cover with cheese and pour over remaining sauce.

- Cook, uncovered, in the oven for 30–35 minutes.

- Serve with a tossed green salad.

Prawns with Garlic, Chilli & Parsley

Serves 4

1 kg (about 20) green prawns, shelled and deveined, tails left intact
2 tablespoons olive oil
1 tablespoon lemon juice
2 cloves garlic, crushed
2 red chillies, deseeded and finely chopped
2 tablespoons chopped fresh parsley
oil for frying
½ cup plain flour
lemon wedges to garnish

- Cut the prawns down the back and remove the vein. Combine the oil, lemon juice, garlic, chillies and parsley in a bowl. Add the prawns, mix well, and leave to marinate for 2–3 hours.

- Heat the oil in a large pan, coat the prawns with flour, and cook quickly in the oil for 2–3 minutes. Drain on absorbent paper.

- Serve with lemon wedges.

Italian Marinara

Serves 6

1kg (2 lb) marinara mix— oysters, scallops, prawns (shrimp), crayfish (all shelled), fish fillet pieces
60 ml (¼ cup) olive oil
2 cloves garlic, sliced
2 x 425 g (1lb 12 oz) tin tomatoes, puréed
1½ teaspoons salt
1 teaspoon oregano
1 teaspoon parsley, chopped
¼ teaspoon freshly ground black pepper
2 tablespoons red wine (optional)
375 g (12 oz) fettucine or spaghetti

🫒 Wash and drain the marinara mix. Heat oil in a large frying pan and sauté marinara mix over a medium heat for 5 minutes. Remove from pan and keep warm.

🫒 Add garlic to the pan and sauté until golden.

🫒 Stir in tomatoes, salt, oregano, parsley, pepper and wine (if using).

- Cook rapidly, uncovered, for 15 minutes, or until sauce has thickened. Stir occasionally.

- If sauce becomes too thick, add ¼–½ cup water.

- Add marinara mix and reheat gently.

- Meanwhile, cook spaghetti in boiling, salted water and drain.

- Serve immediately with marinara sauce poured on top.

Originating most likely in Naples as a simple flatbread, what we think of as 'pizza' is only one member of a family of traditional Italian bread-based foods that serve as a meal in one.

The best pizzas all have one thing in common: they are made from the best quality ingredients.

Use a good grade of olive oil for pizza dough and cooked sauces. Save the finest grades (virgin or extra-virgin) for drizzling over pizza just before baking.

Use the best-quality cheese. Buy a block of aged Parmesan (not pre-grated (shredded)) and grate (shred) it just before using.

Use fresh whole mozzarella cheese packed in its own whey, if available; otherwise use a premium brand of packaged whole mozzarella (not pre-sliced or pre-grated).

Use fresh herbs when possible; if you use dried herbs, purchase them in small quantities.

Use fresh garlic, prepared shortly before using.

Neapolitan pizza dough

Makes 1 pizza crust

7 g (¼ oz) dry yeast
300 ml (½ pint/1¼ cups) warm water (about
41°C/105°F)
275 g (10 oz/2½ cups) plain (all-purpose) flour
½ teaspoon salt

🫒 In a medium bowl dissolve the yeast in the water.
Add half of the flour and mix well to make a sponge
or soft batter-like dough. Cover with cling wrap
(cling film) and leave to rise for about 45 minutes.

🫒 In a large bowl, combine the remaining flour and
the salt. Add the risen dough and mix well. Turn
out onto a lightly floured surface and knead until
smooth and silky (about 5 minutes), adding flour as
necessary.

🫒 Put the dough in an oiled bowl and turn to coat
evenly.

- Cover and leave to rise for 2 hours.

- Punch down the dough using your fist in a straight-down motion.

- To shape into pizza crust, on lightly floured surface, roll out the dough to the desired size. Place on a baker's peel or oiled pizza pan dusted with cornmeal. Any excess dough can be wrapped in plastic kitchen wrap and kept in the refrigerator.

NOTE:

This classic Neapolitan pizza dough yields a dry crisp crust that can support a moist topping, such as fresh clams. The recipe contains no oil other than which is used for oiling the bowl and the dough prior to rising. Allowing the dough to rise twice produces a better taste.

Food processor pizza dough

Makes 1 pizza crust

275 g (10 oz/2½ cups) plain (all-purpose) flour
7 g (¼ oz) fast-rising active dry yeast
¼ teaspoon salt
250 ml (8 fl oz/1 cup) very warm water
(about 50°C/ 122°F)
1 teaspoon honey
2 teaspoons olive oil

- In the bowl of a food processor fitted with a steel blade, mix the flour, yeast and salt. Combine the water, honey and olive oil in a measuring cup.

- With the processor running, pour the water mixture through the feed tube in a steady stream, adjusting the amount poured so the flour can absorb it. Turn the processor off when the dough gathers into clumps and before it forms a smooth ball.

- Do not over process – it should feel sticky. If it is too soft, add more flour, 1 tablespoon at a time, until the dough has a firm consistency.

- Knead by processing for an additional 45 seconds or knead by hand until the dough is smooth and silky. Shape into a ball.

- Place the dough in an oiled bowl and turn to coat evenly. Cover with cling wrap (cling film) and leave to rise in a warm place until doubled in bulk (30–40 minutes).

- Punch down the dough, cover with the inverted bowl, let rest for 10 minutes.

- To shape into pizza crust, on lightly floured surface, roll the dough out to the desired size.

- Place on the baker's peel or oiled pizza pan dusted with cornmeal.

- Any excess dough can be wrapped in plastic kitchen wrap and kept in the refrigerator.

Basic Tomato Sauce

Makes 120 ml (4 fl oz/½ cup)

3 tablespoons chopped fresh basil
½ teaspoon dried oregano
1½ tablespoons white wine
¼ medium onion, grated (shredded)
1 clove garlic, chopped
1 teaspoon olive oil
2 tomatoes peeled, deseeded and chopped
1½ teaspoons tomato paste (purée)

🍒 In a small bowl, steep (infuse) the basil and oregano in white wine for 10 minutes.

🍒 In a pan over medium-high heat, sauté the onion and garlic in olive oil for 5 minutes, stirring frequently. Add the tomatoes and tomato paste, then the herbs and wine. Cover, reduce the heat and simmer for 15 minutes.

🍒 Remove the sauce from the heat and purée in a blender or food processor.

Pizza Parma

1 quantity basic pizza dough

115 g (4 oz) prosciutto, thinly sliced
2 red capsicums (bell peppers), roasted and sliced
45 g (1½ oz) mozzarella cheese, grated (shredded)
45 g (1½ oz) Parmesan, grated (shredded)
¼ cup flat leaf parsley, finely chopped
olive oil

Preheat the oven to 230°C/450°F/Gas mark 8.

- Shape the pizza dough, roll out into a round and fit on a lightly greased baking tray (sheet).

- Arrange slices of prosciutto on the surface of the dough. Add the capsicums and cover with mozzarella, Parmesan and parsley. Drizzle olive oil over the surface.

- Bake until well-browned and puffy, depending on how hot your oven is , it should be between 15-20 minutes or until crispy and brown.

Gorgonzola & Prosciutto pizza

Makes 1 pizza

3 cloves garlic, unpeeled
1 quantity basic pizza dough
1 quantity basic tomato sauce
200 g (7 oz) mozzarella cheese, grated (shredded)
45 g (1½ oz) crumbled Gorgonzola cheese
115 g (4 oz) sliced prosciutto, cut into strips

Preheat the oven to 230°C/450°F/Gas mark 8.

- Add the garlic to 475 ml (16 fl oz/2 cups) boiling water in a small saucepan, boil for 1 minute. Drain, peel, then thinly slice.

- Shape the pizza dough and spread the sauce over the dough. Sprinkle with garlic, then with the cheeses. Arrange the prosciutto strips over the top.

- Bake until the crust is well-browned, 15–20 minutes.

Pumpkin pizza

1 quantity basic pizza dough

½ cup basic tomato sauce
100 g (3½ oz) pumpkin, diced and roasted
55 g (2 oz) feta cheese, crumbled
2 sprigs mint, chopped

- Preheat the oven to 180°C/350°F/Gas mark 4.

- Divide the pizza dough in two and roll out each piece to make two small pizza bases.

- Spread each with tomato sauce. Top with the roasted pumpkin, feta and mint.

- Bake for 15–20 minutes until golden brown.

Mushroom pizza

1 quantity basic pizza dough

1 tablespoon olive oil
300 g (10 oz) salsa
1 onion, sliced
85 g (3 oz) mushrooms, sliced
85 g (3 oz) mature Cheddar cheese, grated (shredded)
salt and freshly ground black pepper
4 sprigs oregano, leaves removed and chopped

🍒 Preheat the oven to 220°C/425°F/Gas mark 7.

🍒 Shape the pizza dought into a 30 cm (12 in) round.

🍒 Place on a lightly greased baking tray (sheet) and
   brush with oil.

🍒 Spread liberally with salsa, then add the onion
   and mushrooms. Drizzle with more olive oil and
   cover liberally with the cheese, salt and pepper and
   oregano.

🍒 Cook for 20–25 minutes, until crispy.

Pancetta & Pear Pizza

1 quantity basic pizza dough

150 g (5 oz) pancetta or prosciutto, thinly sliced
1 firm pear, cored, peeled and sliced
115 g (4 oz) creamy blue cheese such as Gorgonzola,
crumbled
55 g (2 oz) walnuts, chopped
115 g (4 oz) rocket (arugula), roughly chopped
2 tablespoons balsamic or red wine vinegar
freshly ground black pepper

- Preheat oven to 200ºC/400ºF/Gas mark 6.

- Divide the dough into four portions and shape each
  to form a 15 cm (6 in) round. Place the rounds on
  lightly greased baking trays (sheets) and cover with
  pancetta or bacon.

- Arrange the pear slices attractively on top of the
  pancetta or prosciutto, then sprinkle with cheese
  and walnuts. Bake for 15–20 minutes or until the
  base is crisp and golden.

- Just prior to serving, toss the rocket with vinegar and
  pile on top of the pizzas. Season to taste with black
  pepper and serve immediately.

Pepperoni Pizza

2 quantities basic pizza dough

150 g (6 oz/⅔) cup tomato paste (purée)
200 g (7 oz) button (white) mushrooms, sliced
1 green capsicum (bell pepper), chopped
20 slices pepperoni
20 slices cabanossi sausage
225 g (8 oz) mozzarella cheese, grated (shredded)

🫒 Preheat the oven to 200°C/400°F/Gas mark 6.

🫒 Prepare the pizza dough, then shape it into two 30 cm (12 in) rounds and place on greased baking trays (sheets). Spread with tomato paste, then top each base with half the mushrooms and capsicum.

🫒 Arrange half the pepperoni and cabanossi sausage on each pizza and scatter each half with mozzarella.

🫒 Bake for 25–30 minutes, or until cheese is golden and base is crisp.

Smoked salmon pizza

1 quantity basic pizza dough

1 tablespoon olive oil
200 g (7 oz) smoked salmon slices
freshly ground black pepper
4 tablespoons crème fraîche or sour cream
4 teaspoons salmon caviar
¼ cup fresh lemon thyme, chopped

- Preheat the oven to 200°C/400°F/Gas mark 6.

- Divide the pizza dough into four portions and shape each to form a 15 cm (6 in) round. Place the rounds on lightly greased baking trays (sheets), brush with oil and bake for 15 minutes or until crisp and golden.

- Reduce the oven temperature to 180°C/350°F/Gas mark

- Top the pizzas with smoked salmon and black pepper, to taste, and bake for 8 minutes or until the salmon is hot.

- Top the pizzas with crème fraîche and caviar and sprinkle with thyme.

Individual egg & bacon pizzas

1 quantity basic pizza dough

1 quantity basic tomato sauce
1 large onion, finely sliced
4 rashers (strips) bacon, cut into small pieces
salt and freshly ground black pepper
4 eggs
30 g (1 oz) Parmesan, grated (shredded)

- Preheat the oven to 220°C/425°F/Gas mark 7.

- Divide the dough into four equal pieces. Roll out each on a lightly floured work surface into a thin round. Place each on a baking tray (sheet).

- Spread about 5 tablespoons of the tomato sauce over each pizza base.

- Scatter the onion over the tomato sauce, then the bacon. Season with salt and pepper.

- Break one egg onto the centre of each pizza. Scatter the cheese evenly over each pizza.

- Bake for about 10–15 minutes. Serve immediately.

Bacon & goat cheese pizza

1 quantity basic pizza dough

1 quantity basic tomato sauce
1 onion, thinly sliced
4 rashers (strips) bacon
50 g (2 oz) goat's cheese
salt and freshly ground black pepper
6 sprigs fresh marjoram, leaves removed and stalks discarded
black olives

- Preheat the oven to 220°C/425°F/Gas mark 7.

- Roll out the dough on a lightly floured work surface. Place on a greased baking tray (sheet).

- Spread the tomato sauce over the dough, then sprinkle over the onion. Cut the bacon into small pieces and scatter over the pizza.

- Thinly slice the goat's cheese and place the slices over the bacon.

- Season with salt and pepper, sprinkle over the marjoram and bake for about 15 minutes. Serve hot, garnished with olives.

Ham & Mozzarella Pizza

1 quantity basic pizza dough

2 tablespoons olive oil
1 onion, finely chopped
4 large tomatoes, skinned and finely chopped
1 bay leaf
1 small sprig thyme
few drops of Tabasco sauce
1 clove garlic, finely chopped
salt and freshly ground black pepper

Topping

2 tomatoes, sliced
½ onion, thinly sliced
2 slices lean cooked ham, diced
200 g (7 oz) mozzarella cheese
salt and freshly ground black pepper
1 teaspoon dried oregano
fresh oregano, chopped

- Preheat the oven to 220°C/425°F/Gas mark 7.

- To make the tomato sauce, heat the oil in a frying pan and fry the onion until softened. Add the tomatoes, bay leaf, thyme, Tabasco and garlic. Season with salt and pepper and cook for about 30 minutes, stirring frequently.

- When the liquid from the tomatoes has almost evaporated, remove and discard the bay leaf and the sprig of thyme. Allow the sauce to cool a little, then blend in a food processor until smooth.

- Roll out the dough into a round, place on a baking tray (sheet) and spread with the prepared tomato sauce.

- Arrange the sliced tomatoes over the tomato sauce, then top with the onion and ham. Cut the cheese into thin slices and scatter over the pizza. Season with salt and pepper and sprinkle over the oregano.

- Bake for 15 minutes. Serve immediately garnished with fresh oregano.

Pizza Galette

Serves 4

7 g (¼ oz) active dry yeast
100 g (3½ oz/½ cup) sugar, plus 5 tablespoons to decorate
115 g (4 oz) butter, softened, plus 30 g (1 oz) to decorate
1 teaspoon lemon zest
1 egg
pinch of salt
200 g (7 oz/1¾ cups) plain (all-purpose) flour
olive oil

🍒 Sprinkle the yeast over the 50 ml (2 fl oz/¼ cup) warm
water in a small bowl.

🍒 Add 1 tablespoon of the sugar. Let stand until the yeast
is soft (about 5 minutes).

🍒 In the bowl of an electric mixer, cream the butter with
2 tablespoons of sugar until fluffy. Blend in the lemon
zest, then the egg.

🍒 Stir the salt into the yeast mixture, then blend into the
butter mixture.

- Gradually blend in the flour to make a soft dough. Continue beating until the dough is smooth and elastic (about 5 minutes).

- Place the dough in a buttered bowl. Cover with cling wrap (cling film) and leave to rise in a warm place until doubled in bulk (about 1½ hours).

- Punch dough down. Roll the dough on a well-floured surface into a circle about 30 cm (12 in) in diameter.

- Preheat the oven to 220°C/425°F/Gas mark 7. Oil a 40 cm (16 in) pizza pan.

- Pat and stretch the dough to fit the pan, pinching the edge to make a slightly raised rim. Cut the remaining 30 g (1oz) butter into 24 equal pieces and distribute evenly over the dough. Sprinkle with the remaining 5 tablespoons of sugar.

- Bake until well browned, 12–15 minutes. Cut into wedges and serve warm.

Tiramisu

Serves 4

3 eggs
100 g (3½ oz) sugar
250 g (8 oz) mascarpone
250 ml (8 fl oz) whipping cream
30 ml (1 fl oz) kahlua or Marsala
500 ml (16 fl oz) strong coffee, lightly sweetened
200 g (6 oz) Ladyfingers biscuits
Unsweetened cocoa powder, for dusting

- Using electric beaters, beat the eggs in a large mixing bowl, then add the sugar and continue mixing until combined . Add the mascarpone and mix until well combined.

- In a separate bowl, whip the fresh cream, then fold it gently into the mascarpone mixture.

- Add the Marsala or kahlua and mix until well combined, then set aside.

- Pour the coffee into a medium bowl and cut the ladyfingers in half.

- Dip them in coffee, one at a time, and allow the coffee to be absorbed.

- Arrange them around the sides of glasses or a bowl.

- Divide the mascarpone mixture evenly between the glasses on top of the fingers.

- Repeat with remaining biscuits and marscapone mixture.

- Dust with cocoa powder and refrigerate for 4 hours before serving.

Index

Baby Octopus Salad	20
Basic Tomato Sauce	106
Beef Carpaccio	26
Cannelloni Stuffed With Ricotta In Tomato Sauce	58
Clam Chowder	66
Cooking Pasta	5
Fettuccine Alfredo	60
Garlic Bread	16
Gnocchi	62
Insalata Caprese	18
Italian Marinara	96
Lasagne	28
Minestrone	22
Mushroom Risotto	78
Mussel Risotto	84
Mussels with Garlic	52
Penne with Pancetta & Tomatoes	40
Penne with Tomato Sauce	36
Pizza: Bacon & goat cheese pizza	119
Pizza: Food processor pizza dough	104
Pizza: Gorgonzola & Prosciutto pizza	110
Pizza: Ham & Mozzarella Pizza	120
Pizza: Individual egg & bacon pizzas	118

Pizza: Mushroom pizza	113
Pizza: Neapolitan pizza dough	102
Pizza: Pancetta & Pear Pizza	114
Pizza: Pepperoni Pizza	115
Pizza: Pizza Galette	122
Pizza: Pumpkin pizza	112
Pizza: Smoked salmon pizza	116
Pizza: Pizza Parma	108
Prawns with Garlic, Chilli & Parsley	94
Ravioli	86
Risotto with Spinach & Gorgonzola	76
Roasted Pumpkin Risotto	72
Seafood Risotto	80
Shrimp Risotto	70
Spaghetti Carbonara	38
Spaghetti Bolognese	46
Spaghetti with Meatballs	48
Spaghetti with Mussels	42
Tiramisu	126
Tomato Toasts with Fresh Basil	12
Tuna and Rice Bake	68
Tuna Lasagne	32
Veal Saltimbocca	56
Veal with Mozzarella	90
Whitebait	54

First published in 2023 by New Holland Publishers, Sydney
Level 1, 178 Fox Valley Road, Wahroonga, 2076, NSW,
Australia

newhollandpublishers.com

A record of this book is held at the National Library of
Australia

ISBN : 9781760795801

Group Managing Director: Fiona Schultz
Designer: Ben Taylor (Taylor Design)
Production Director: Arlene Gippert
Printed in China

10 9 8 7 6 5 4 3 2 1

Keep up with New Holland Publishers

f NewHollandPublishers

◎ @newhollandpublishers